# DANCES f

MW01130951

**BOOK 2**

## 5 Intermediate Piano Duets in Dance Styles

# CATHERINE ROLLIN

The pieces in *Dances for Two, Books 1 and 2,* were inspired by a duet recital held at the Goshen College Piano Workshop in Goshen, Indiana, in the summer of 1999. The concert featured student and teacher performances and included a duet that I was commissioned to write for the event, *Valse Sentimentale à Deux.* All of the performers played beautifully, including a professional duet team who played three exciting Cuban dances. Their performance of this dance music was so energetic that I felt like getting up and dancing right at my seat! The concert concluded with my piece performed by two students who played with beautiful unity and really captured the elegance of the waltz. The idea struck me that there is nothing more wonderful for a duet team than to feel like they are dancing at the keyboard with their favorite partner! I dedicated the pieces in *Dances for Two, Books 1 and 2,* to valued colleagues and musicians whose friendship and music making have enriched my life. These are people whom I have met through my work as a composer. Just as duet playing leads to new friendships, I have learned from these people how music brings people together. I hope that playing these pieces will give many duet teams the pleasure of making music together and sharing the special experience of musical friendships!

*Catherine Rollin*

Alfred

*for the wonderful duet teams of Magdalena Nogueras and Arturo Castro, and Ruth Neville and Daniel Koppelman*
*Thank you for your electric rhythm and the vitality of your playing.*

# 1920s Charleston

## SECONDO

Catherine Rollin

**Upbeat, lively and fun!**

*for the wonderful duet teams of Magdalena Nogueras and Arturo Castro, and Ruth Neville and Daniel Koppelman*
*Thank you for your electric rhythm and the vitality of your playing.*

# 1920s CHARLESTON
## PRIMO

Catherine Rollin

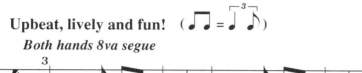

4

SECONDO

SECONDO

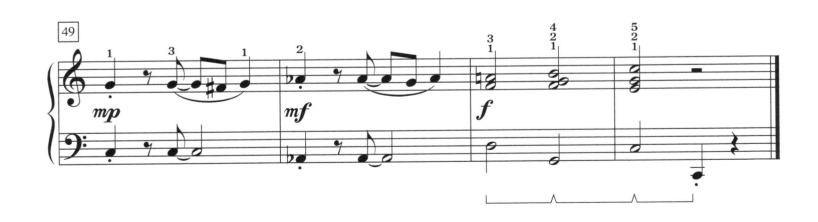

PRIMO

*for Barbara and Gerhardt Suhrstedt*
*Thank you for your friendship and your beautiful and elegant duet performances.*
*You have done so much to bring the joy of duets to people around the world.*

# RUSSIAN WALTZ

## SECONDO

Catherine Rollin

*for Barbara and Gerhardt Suhrstedt*
*Thank you for your friendship and your beautiful and elegant duet performances.*
*You have done so much to bring the joy of duets to people around the world.*

# RUSSIAN WALTZ

## PRIMO

Catherine Rollin

12

SECONDO

*for the Midland Michigan Music Teachers Association*
*Thank you for supporting and celebrating duet music at your annual Keyboardfest.*

# POLKA PARTY
## SECONDO

Catherine Rollin

**Very lively and full of fun!**

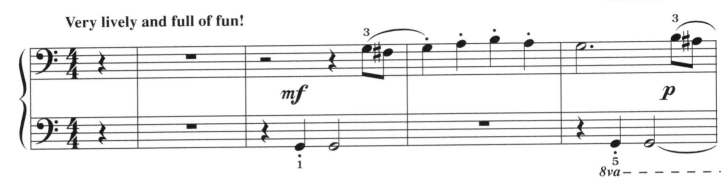

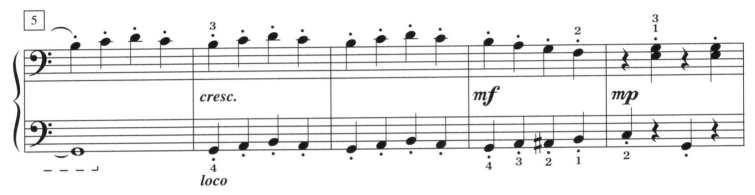

*for the Midland Michigan Music Teachers Association*
*Thank you for supporting and celebrating duet music at your annual Keyboardfest.*

# POLKA PARTY

PRIMO

Catherine Rollin

**Very lively and full of fun!**

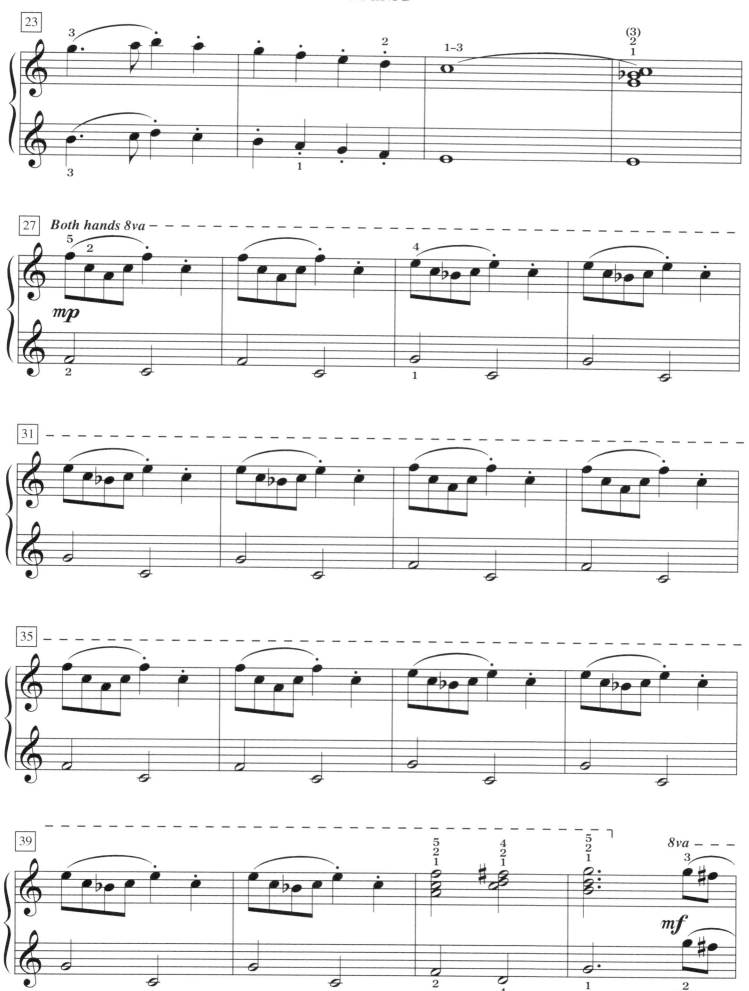

SECONDO

*for Ingrid Jacobson Clarfield—Thank you for sharing your passion for piano, teaching, duets and life.*
*for Yuki and Tomoko Mack—Thank you for your duet artistry and dedication to American music.*

# SQUARE DANCE U.S.A.!

## SECONDO

Catherine Rollin

*for Ingrid Jacobson Clarfield—Thank you for sharing your passion for piano, teaching, duets and life.*
*for Yuki and Tomoko Mack—Thank you for your duet artistry and dedication to American music.*

# SQUARE DANCE U.S.A.!
## PRIMO

**With a robust spirit and lots of energy**

*Both hands 1 octave higher than written throughout*

Catherine Rollin

SECONDO

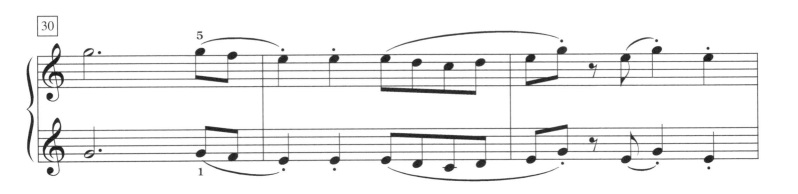

24

## SECONDO

*for Morty and Iris Manus—a great duet in life!*
*Thank you for your warmth and support over the years.*

# GOOD, OLD-FASHIONED ROCK AND ROLL
## SECONDO

Catherine Rollin

*for Morty and Iris Manus—a great duet in life!*
*Thank you for your warmth and support over the years.*

# GOOD, OLD-FASHIONED ROCK AND ROLL
## PRIMO

Catherine Rollin

SECONDO

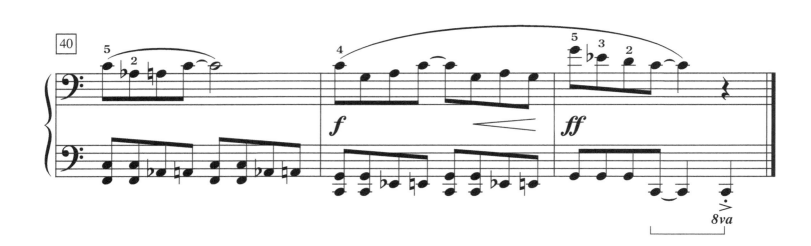

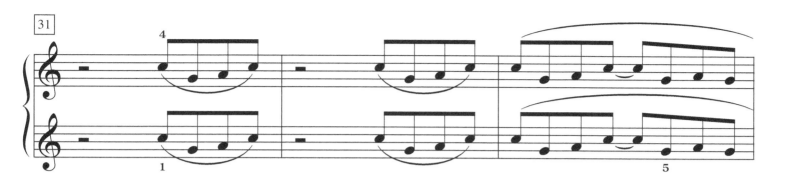

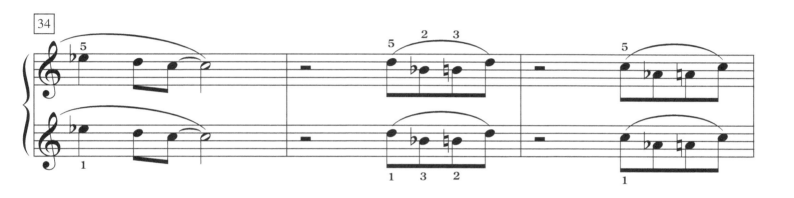